W9-CYX-901

DISNEY
LEARNING

DISNEY
QUIZ MAGIC

DISNEY · PIXAR

TOY STORY

QUIZZES

GIDDYUP,
PARTNER!

JENNIFER BOOTHROYD

LERNER PUBLICATIONS ◆ MINNEAPOLIS

For David and Lauren

Mark your quiz answers on a separate sheet of paper.
Then check your answers when you're finished with the quiz!

Lerner Publications Company
A division of Lerner Publishing Group, Inc.
241 First Avenue North
Minneapolis, MN 55401 USA

For reading levels and more information, look up this title
at www.lernerbooks.com.

Main body text set in Avenir LT Pro and ITC Lubalin Graph Std.
Typefaces provided by Linotype AG and International Typeface Corp.

Library of Congress Cataloging-in-Publication Data

Names: Boothroyd, Jennifer, 1972– author.
Title: Toy story quizzes : giddyup, partner! / Jennifer Boothroyd.
Description: Minneapolis : Lerner Publications, 2019. | Series: Disney quiz
   magic | Includes bibliographical references.
Identifiers: LCCN 2018046572 (print) | LCCN 2018055287 (ebook) |
   ISBN 9781541561526 (eb pdf) | ISBN 9781541554764 (lb : alk. paper)
Subjects: LCSH: Toy story (Motion pictures)—Miscellanea—Juvenile
   literature.
Classification: LCC PN1997.T654 (ebook) | LCC PN1997.T654 B66 2019 (print) |
   DDC 791.43/72—dc23

LC record available at https://lccn.loc.gov/2018046572

Manufactured in the United States of America
1-45794-42676-1/17/2019

TABLE OF CONTENTS

THE WORLD OF TOY STORY

TOY STORY FANS AROUND THE WORLD KNOW WOODY, JESSIE, BUZZ, BO PEEP, AND THE REST OF THE GANG. Their stories of friendship and teamwork have touched the hearts of billions.

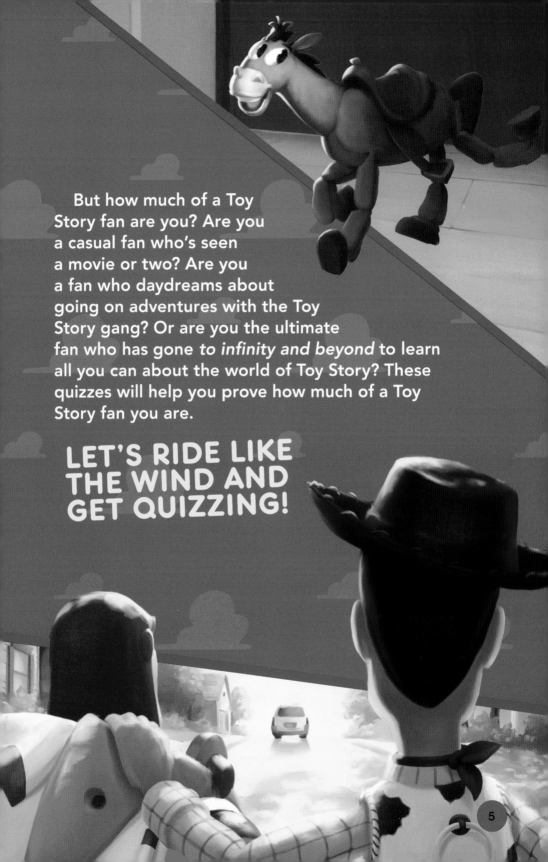

But how much of a Toy Story fan are you? Are you a casual fan who's seen a movie or two? Are you a fan who daydreams about going on adventures with the Toy Story gang? Or are you the ultimate fan who has gone *to infinity and beyond* to learn all you can about the world of Toy Story? These quizzes will help you prove how much of a Toy Story fan you are.

LET'S RIDE LIKE THE WIND AND GET QUIZZING!

WHICH TOY STORY TOY WOULD YOU PLAY WITH THE MOST?

1. Which of these toy features is your favorite?

    A. a cloth body
    B. a voice box
    C. some tires
    D. posable arms and legs

2. Do you like noisy toys?

    A. No.
    B. Noises are fun.
    C. The louder the better!
    D. A little squeak is okay.

3. Which type of toy do you like best?

A. dolls
B. action figures
C. cars
D. stuffed animals

4. What is the one thing you look for in a toy?

A. toys that are huggable
B. toys with moving parts
C. toys with controllers
D. toys that don't break easily

5. Which color combination do you like best?

A. purple and orange
B. green and white
C. green and blue
D. purple and blue

6. What kind of toys are your favorite?

A. one-of-a-kind toys
B. new toys
C. high-tech toys
D. classic toys

TURN THE PAGE FOR ANSWERS!

STORYTELLING SPOTLIGHT

A story's tone affects how the audience feels. Stories can be serious, funny, sad, or hopeful. What is the tone of your favorite Toy Story movie?

THE TOY YOU WOULD PLAY WITH IS . . .

IF YOU ANSWERED MOSTLY As, Dolly is the toy for you. She's soft, sassy, and a great listener.

IF YOU ANSWERED MOSTLY Bs, Buzz Lightyear is the toy for you. He's built for action.

IF YOU ANSWERED MOSTLY Cs, RC is the toy for you. He's a speedy machine that's ready to roll.

IF YOU ANSWERED MOSTLY Ds, Trixie is the toy for you. She's tough enough to take on any adventure.

•• ANDY'S TOYS: TRUE OR FALSE?

1. GREEN ARMY MEN WERE ANDY'S TOYS.

2. MR. PRICKLEPANTS WAS ANDY'S TOY.

3. HAMM WAS ANDY'S TOY.

4. ROLLER BOB WAS ANDY'S TOY.

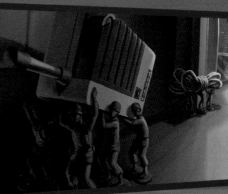

COMPARE/CONTRAST

Buzz and Woody don't always agree, but they are very good friends. How are Buzz and Woody similar? How are they different?

1. True. 2. False. He's Bonnie's toy. 3. True. 4. False. He's Sid's creation.

WHERE DID WE FIRST MEET THESE TOY STORY CHARACTERS?

1. **Where did we first meet Jessie?**
   A. Andy's house
   B. Second Chance Antiques
   C. Bonnie's house
   D. Al's apartment

2. **Where did we first meet Giggle McDimples?**
   A. Andy's house
   B. Sunnyside Daycare
   C. a playground in Grand Basin
   D. Al's apartment

3. Where did we first meet Buttercup?

  A. Second Chance Antiques

  B. Sunnyside Daycare

  C. Bonnie's house

  D. Al's apartment

4. Where did we first meet Wheezy?

  A. Andy's house

  B. Sunnyside Daycare

  C. Bonnie's house

  D. Al's apartment

STORYTELLING SPOTLIGHT

The setting is where a story takes place. It can help set the mood. How would you describe Sunnyside Daycare at the beginning, the middle, and the end of *Toy Story 3*?

✿WHAT ROLE WOULD YOU PLAY IN BONNIE'S STORIES?

1. Your friends think you are
   A. brave
   B. sneaky
   C. goofy
   D. loyal

2. You like to
   A. protect others from harm
   B. be in charge
   C. perform for an audience
   D. compliment others

3. Your dentist thinks you

    A. are a good brusher

    B. bite too hard

    C. have a big smile

    D. need to open wider

4. Which is your favorite Toy Story movie?

    A. *Toy Story*

    B. *Toy Story 2*

    C. *Toy Story 3*

    D. *Toy Story 4*

5. Your teacher thinks you are

    A. a leader

    B. a genius

    C. a clown

    D. a friend

6. What kind of party food do you like best?

    A. something unusual

    B. something spicy

    C. something sugary

    D. something healthy

TURN THE PAGE FOR ANSWERS!

CHARACTER CONNECTION

Bonnie is very creative. She uses her imagination to play with her toys in different ways. How do you show your creativity and imagination? Why is creativity important?

YOUR ROLE WOULD BE . . .

IF YOU ANSWERED MOSTLY As, you'd play the hero. Heroes like Woody, Buzz, and Jessie often have to make tough choices when saving the day.

IF YOU ANSWERED MOSTLY Bs, you'd play the villain. Zurg and Stinky Pete might be evil or just misunderstood. Either way, they give the heroes something to fight for. It can be fun playing the bad side sometimes.

IF YOU ANSWERED MOSTLY Cs, you'd play the goofball. Silly characters like Rex and Ducky and Bunny make a story lots of fun.

IF YOU ANSWERED MOSTLY Ds, you'd play the helpful sidekick. Heroes and villains depend on their sidekicks to reach their goals. Woody needs Bullseye, just like Lotso needs Big Baby.

SID THE TOY MAKER: TRUE OR FALSE?

1. SID MADE HIS BABYHEAD TOY FROM A DOLL AND A CONSTRUCTION SET.

2. SID MADE A TOY CALLED BLOCKFEET FROM WOODEN BLOCKS AND A STUFFED ANIMAL.

3. SID MADE THE FLYING LOCO TOY FROM A TRAIN SET AND A BUZZ LIGHTYEAR.

4. SID MADE A NEW TOY NAMED LEGS FROM A DOLL AND A FISHING ROD.

COMPARE/CONTRAST

Andy and Sid are very different characters, but even opposites are alike in some ways. What are some things that make Andy and Sid different? What do Andy and Sid have in common?

1. True. 2. False. Sid never made a toy like that. 3. False. That sounds cool but doesn't exist. 4. True.

NAME THAT CHARACTER!

1. **What does Buttercup call Mr. Pricklepants?**

   A. Baron Von Shush

   B. Daddy

   C. Ned

   D. Mr. Lederhosen

2. **What are the names of Bo Peep's sheep?**

   A. Huey, Dewey, and Louie

   B. Ba, Baa, and Baaa

   C. Billy, Goat, and Gruff

   D. Fuzzy, Fluffy, and Frizzy

3. Who plays Mrs. Nesbitt in Hannah's room?
   A. Mrs. Potato Head
   B. Buzz Lightyear
   C. Bo Peep
   D. Hamm

4. What is the name of Bo Peep's daredevil friend?
   A. Canada Carl
   B. Forky
   C. Duke Caboom
   D. Lightning McQueen

STORYTELLING SPOTLIGHT

Dialogue is what the characters say in a story. What can you learn about the characters from their dialogue? What are some of your favorite Toy Story quotes?

1.A; 2.C; 3.B; 4.C

17

✪WHICH TOY STORY ADVENTURE IS FOR YOU?

1. Would you rather . . .
 A. work on a project with old friends
 B. work on a project on a large team
 C. work on a project with a partner
 D. work on a project with new friends

2. Would you rather . . .
   A. jump
   B. walk
   C. ride in a vehicle
   D. be carried

3. Would you rather . . .
   A. bungee jump
   B. go camping
   C. skydive
   D. drive a big truck

4. Would you rather . . .
   A. be outside in the rain
   B. be outside on a hot, sunny day
   C. be outside at night
   D. be outside in the shade

5. Would you rather . . .
   A. sleep until noon
   B. wake up before sunrise
   C. stay up past midnight
   D. take an afternoon nap

6. Would you rather . . .
   A. be a doll
   B. be a rocket
   C. be a horse
   D. be a crayon

TURN THE PAGE FOR ANSWERS!

CHARACTER CONNECTION

Buzz, Woody, and the Toy Story gang aren't perfect. But self-reflection helps them learn from their mistakes. When was the last time you made a big mistake? What did you learn from that mistake?

THE ADVENTURE YOU SHOULD GO ON IS . . .

IF YOU ANSWERED MOSTLY As, rescuing RC from the driveway is your kind of adventure. Nothing will stop you from helping a friend.

IF YOU ANSWERED MOSTLY Bs, stopping Sid from destroying his toys is the adventure for you. You enjoy being on a large team to make life better for others.

IF YOU ANSWERED MOSTLY Cs, escaping an airplane is your perfect adventure. Working together, like Woody and Jessie do, is how you want to get things done.

IF YOU ANSWERED MOSTLY Ds, moving to Bonnie's house is an adventure made for you. You are excited to meet new people and see new places.

WHO SAID IT: REX OR TRIXIE?

1. "I JUST CAME BACK FROM THE DOCTOR WITH LIFE-CHANGING NEWS."

2. "BUT LOOK AT MY LITTLE ARMS! I CAN'T PRESS THE FIRE BUTTON AND JUMP AT THE SAME TIME!"

3. "HOW DO YOU SPELL 'FBI'?"

4. "WE'RE EITHER IN A CAFÉ IN PARIS OR A COFFEE SHOP IN NEW JERSEY."

5. "THAT'S JUST A DINOSAUR TOY DOWN THE STREET."

COMPARE/CONTRAST

Besides both being dinosaurs, what do Trixie and Rex have in common? How are they different from each other?

ARE YOU A TOY STORY EXPERT?

1. Who was Jessie's first kid?
   - A. Cassie
   - B. Emily
   - C. Bonnie
   - D. Molly

2. Which of these is not one of Woody's pull-string phrases?
   - A. "There's a snake in my boot."
   - B. "You're my favorite deputy!"
   - C. "Somebody's poisoned the water hole!"
   - D. "Ride like the wind!"

3. **What had Al been eating when he falls asleep in front of the television?**

A. cheese puffs
B. chips
C. popcorn
D. cookies

4. **Who is the only one Buster follows commands from?**

A. Andy
B. Molly
C. Woody
D. Hamm

5. **What is Giggle McDimples's job?**

A. Pet Patrol Officer
B. Mini-opolis Mall Security Guard
C. Animal Aid Associate
D. Missing Toys Detective

COMPARE/CONTRAST

Andy changes a lot in the ten years between *Toy Story* and *Toy Story 3*. Imagine yourself ten years from now. What do you think the world will be like? What will you be like?

●WHICH TOY FROM TOY STORY ARE YOU?

1. **What do you do in a group of people?**
   A. take charge of the group
   B. become the center of attention
   C. entertain them
   D. make sure everyone feels welcome

2. **Which of these makes you the most excited?**
   A. friends
   B. traveling
   C. animals
   D. adventures

3. **Which of these things would you most like to do?**

A. plan activities for your friends
B. learn to speak two languages
C. dance your heart out
D. make new friends

4. **Which adjective describes your best friend?**

A. loud
B. organized
C. caring
D. helpful

5. **Which accessory do you like best?**

A. belt
B. gloves
C. boots
D. hat

6. **Pick a color.**

A. brown
B. purple
C. red
D. pink

TURN THE PAGE FOR ANSWERS!

CHARACTER CONNECTION

Friendship is at the heart of the Toy Story movies. Why are your friends important to you? What do you do to show your friends you care about them?

YOU ARE . . .

IF YOU ANSWERED MOSTLY As, you are Woody. He is a loyal friend and a good leader.

IF YOU ANSWERED MOSTLY Bs, you are Buzz. He is motivated to get things done and helps his friends.

IF YOU ANSWERED MOSTLY Cs, you are Jessie. She loves animals and keeps her friends entertained.

IF YOU ANSWERED MOSTLY Ds, you are Bo Peep. She has an independent spirit and is a caring friend.

SECOND CHANCE: TRUE OR FALSE?

1. ALL THE TOYS AT SECOND CHANCE ANTIQUES ARE BROKEN.

2. GABBY GABBY, BO PEEP, AND DUKE CABOOM ALL SPENT TIME AT THE STORE.

3. HARMONY'S MOTHER OWNS SECOND CHANCE ANTIQUES.

4. TOYS AT SECOND CHANCE ANTIQUES NEED TO WATCH OUT FOR DRAGON THE CAT.

STORYTELLING SPOTLIGHT

Main characters are the focus of a story. The other characters are important because they help move the story along. Why are characters like Ducky and Bunny, Giggle McDimples, and Duke Caboom important to *Toy Story 4*?

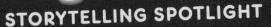

1. False. Only some of the toys are broken. 2. True. 3. False. Harmony's grandmother owns the store. 4. True.

MAKE YOUR OWN QUIZ!

DO YOU WANT TO TEST YOUR FRIENDS AND FAMILY ON THEIR TOY STORY KNOWLEDGE? Make a copy of the blank quiz on the next page, and create your own Toy Story quiz. You could ask about the Toy Story villains or the human characters in Toy Story. Your friends will be *eternally grateful* that you shared your love of Toy Story.

MY

QUIZ:

_____

1. _____

   A. _____

   B. _____

   C. _____

   D. _____

2. _____

   A. _____

   B. _____

   C. _____

   D. _____

3. _____

   A. _____

   B. _____

   C. _____

   D. _____

FUN FACTS

There are more than a million monkeys released during the barrel explosion in *Toy Story 3*.

In 2008, astronauts took a Buzz Lightyear action figure into space.

John Ratzenberger is the voice of Hamm in the Toy Story movies. He's been in all twenty-one Pixar movies.

Animators strapped wooden boards to their feet as they were trying to figure out how the Green Army Men would walk. It was harder to move than they thought!

TO LEARN MORE

BOOKS

Boothroyd, Jennifer. *How to be a Beloved Toy: Teamwork with Woody*. Minneapolis: Lerner Publications, 2019.
Follow the adventures of Woody and the Toy Story gang as they use teamwork to be the best toys.

Lindeen, Mary. *Toy Story Top 10s: To Infinity and Beyond*. Minneapolis: Lerner Publications, 2019.
Check out this book to read all about the top lines, moments, and more from the Toy Story movies.

WEBSITES

Disney Family: Our Favorite Toy Story Crafts and Recipes
https://family.disney.com/articles/our-favorite-toy-story-crafts-and-recipes/
Celebrate your love of the Toy Story characters by making these cool crafts and yummy recipes.

Disney Pixar: Toy Story
https://toystory.disney.com/
Dive into the world of Toy Story. Watch clips from the movies. Play games with Woody or Buzz. Learn more about the characters by reading their bios.